Life and Times of Napoleon J. Dyer

By
Attorney
Rodney N. Dyer

Life and Times of Napoleon J. Dyer
By
Attorney Rodney N. Dyer

Copyright © 2022 by Rodney N. Dyer. All rights reserved.

Copyright © 2022 illustrations by Courtney Parsons. All rights reserved.

This book or any portion thereof may not be reproduced or used in any manner whatsoever without the express written permission of the publisher except for the use of brief quotations in a book review.

Library of Congress Control Number: 2022943678

Paperback ISBN: 979-8-9854340-5-7

Book Cover Design and Layout: Pamela Marin-Kingsley

Book Editor: Jane Stucker

Give a Salute! provides publishing services to the author(s) specifications and approval. The author retains all responsibilities and rights to the content of this book.

Contact for More Information:

GIVE A SALUTE!
Laconia, NH
giveasalute@gmail.com
www.giveasalute.com

Belknap Mill
ARTS • HISTORY • EDUCATION

While this book depicts in part the life and times of my great grandfather, Napoleon J. Dyer, it might also be a metaphor for the struggles and aspirations of French Canadians, Irish, Jewish, and other immigrants to New Hampshire in the late 19th century. Dedication is to those NH families and their descendants who now enjoy the American Way.

Napoleon was an interesting person. His story began as a presentation to the Laconia Historical and Museum Society and morphed into a book at the suggestion of the Belknap Mill Society. I give my thanks and appreciation to Warren Huse, Lynn Brody Keltz, Cathy Waldron, and Give a Salute! for their guidance and assistance in this book becoming a reality. Any errors, large or small, have been made by my striving to faithfully recreate the life and times of Napoleon J. Dyer.

In 1874, a young French-Canadian named Napoleon Dionne arrived in Lake Village (Lakeport) by train. He was penniless and virtually illiterate. Up until around 1880, with the exception of a few months, he had no "schooling." He couldn't read an article in a newspaper unless he had a prior knowledge of the subject matter.

Napoleon left his family in Franklin where he had worked as a 13-year-old in the local paper mill, a weaver in a woolen mill, and a dyer in the Sawyer Mill. While working in the mills in Franklin, young Dyer also partially learned the barber trade by working as an apprentice in his spare time.

When this young man came to Lake Village, he was typical of thousands of French Canadians seeking jobs in the New England factories. He called himself Napoleon Dionne, but his true family name was Dionne d' Sansoucy. Dionne was the family surname, and the habit of adding a "dit" developed in France as a means of distinguishing the individual members of a particular family. The original French ancestor of all of the Dionne families was Antoine Dionne d'Sans-soucy (1641 -1721), who came to New France in 1664, or perhaps a little earlier. Sans-soucy is a descriptive term which in French means "easy come, easy go," or "with a devil may care" attitude. The dit was often used to modify a particular family name. It was not a replacement for an existing name but rather an extension of the name; in essence, a double family name which helped to distinguish one person or family from others who had the same surname. The use of dit names has largely disappeared.

Due to the generous assistance of Frank Binette and Lynn Brody Keltz, we are now able to trace the ancestry of this young French-Canadian back to French landholders in the 1600s. As a matter of fact, it is particularly easy to trace the history of many French-Canadian families because the records of births, deaths and marriages were meticulously kept by village priests.

According to newspaper accounts, Napoleon was born on May 24, 1858, in Troy, New York. In actuality, Napoleon was born in Montmagny, Quebec, in 1856 or 1858. This small city is located on the shore of the St. Lawrence River, east of Quebec City, and was founded 350 years ago. Many French Canadians adopted border communities such as Troy, New York, as a "birth place of convenience," so that they would not be classed as illegal immigrants.

Napoleon went to work in the dye house of Robert Appleton in Lake Village and became a dyer by trade. Within a year of his arrival, Napoleon moved from Lake Village into the Town of Laconia, looking for better opportunities. He obtained employment as a weaver in the the mill owned by William Marshall, and remained there until 1881. During this period, he lived in a rooming house on Rowe Court. It was typical that the mill hands would live within walking distance of their employment.

It was during this period of Napoleon's life that he met a young Irish Catholic girl by the name of Mary Jane McLoud. The marital records of the St. Joseph Church indicate a marriage ceremony took place on September 16, 1878, between Napoleon Dion and Mary Jane McLoud. In all probability, the priest at St. Joseph's Church spelled Napoleon's last name phonetically as "Dion," rather than as "Dionne." Five children were born of this marriage, which lasted 65 years, until Napoleon's death in 1943.

Franco-Americans arrived in Meredith Bridge (later Laconia) around 1848 to help build the railroad, and a number of them stayed. In succeeding years, more Franco-Americans came to settle in the Laconia area drawn by employment in the mills. By the end of the century, the then City of Laconia contained a significant Franco-American population. It was during the late 19th century that the names of many French-Canadian immigrants were anglicized either by town officials or often by priests in Irish Catholic parishes. French surnames such as Descoteau became Hill, Roy became Ware or King, Michel became Mitchell, Bernier became Barney, Boncoeur became Bunker, and Fortier became Foote.

The oral history of our family is that when Napoleon applied for employment at at a local mill, he was asked for his name, and he mistakenly thought he was being asked about his trade. Therefore, the name "Dyer" became his name. Thus, it is not surprising that the young man named Napoleon Dionne became Napoleon Dion, and shortly thereafter became Napoleon Dyer. He legally changed his name on December 17, 1889.

According to Frank Binette, many French-speaking immigrants were eager to assimilate and were apprehensive about government authority. Thus, they would not protest when the spelling of their names was corrupted or anglicized. The change from the French-sounding surname ("Dionne") to the English-sounding surname ("Dyer") was therefore consistent with the Franco-American experience in New Hampshire in the late 19th century.

It was during his time in the Belknap Mill that one of the most fascinating aspects of Napoleon's life occurred. It is obvious that he was a very bright individual and that he had a very inquisitive mind, yet he was illiterate. Napoleon later recounted that he learned to read and write while working in the mills because fellow workers would chalk letters and words on the cloth as it was being manufactured. Napoleon subsequently obtained a child's primer and a dictionary and taught himself how to read by pronouncing the words. He graduated to other books as recounted in an article about Napoleon that appeared in the Citizen:

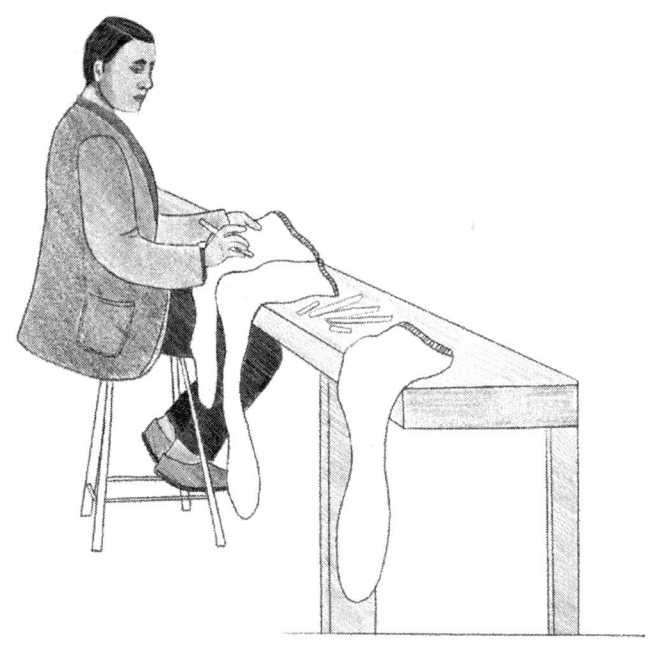

WHATNOT

Noting in the Evening Citizen comments on the polished diction of Attorney N. J. Dyer, Miss Claribel Clark of Lakeport recalls the time when calling at the Lewis mansion off Court Street, now used as a rooming house, she would meet Mr. Dyer coming out with books under his arms, after he had been coached in English by Miss Winnie Lewis, niece of the late Edwin C. Lewis, owner and publisher of the original Laconia Democrat. Miss Lewis and her mother resided at the Lewis home.

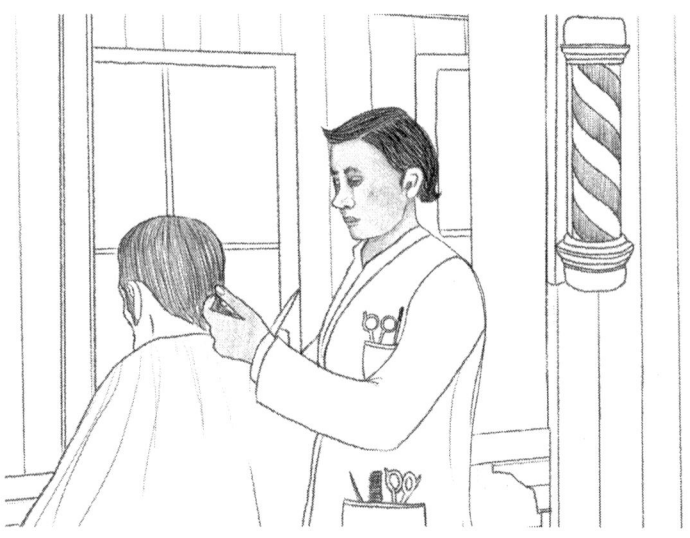

In the meantime, evenings and spare hours, Napoleon had learned something of the barber's trade. In 1881, he bought out a barbershop in Laconia for $50.00 and carried on a successful business for eight years. At the time he acquired the shop, he was married, had two children, and had never attended a school of any kind. His work as a barber brought him in touch with business and professional men. He could see the advantage of having some learning so he was determined to get an education. Later in life, he talked at length with Judge Oscar Young and told of the difficulties he had experienced and the help he received from such men as Judge Charles Stone, E.P. Jewell and Stephen S. Jewett, eminent lawyers, of whom he always spoke in the highest terms.

According to Judge Young, "Napoleon began with a child's primer and when he could read, every night after work, no matter how late, he read aloud for two hours with a dictionary at hand, and never passed a word he did not know, always looking it up and learning its meaning and pronunciation." Napoleon continued the practice of looking up the spelling and definition of words for many years. I have in my possession a spelling dictionary stamped by Napoleon on March 27, 1917. As was his custom, Napoleon had lightly marked items in the margin, and it was obvious that he was methodically going through the book word for word to make certain that he could correctly spell each one and knew its definition.

Judge Young stated that Napoleon was a great reader of history and of the Bible, and few teachers were better informed on important historical events, especially government matters; few Bible students could quote the scriptures more accurately or more at length. It was during this period of his life that he took extension courses through the Chautauqua organization and obtained the equivalent of a college education. He was very interested in a number of fields, including science and medicine, history, religion and politics. These interests would remain with him for the rest of his life.

During his barbering days, Napoleon became acquainted with Judge Charles F. Stone who, at the time, was in partnership with E. Perry Jewell in the firm of Jewell & Stone. Napoleon enjoyed discussing the law with Judge Stone to the extent that the judge eventually asked him one day, "Napoleon, since you enjoy discussing the law so much, why don't you become a lawyer?"

And so it began. For the next five years, Napoleon continued to operate the barbershop in order to support his family, but he spent every spare moment reading the law in the law offices of Col. Stephen Jewett and later in the offices of Jewell & Stone. In the 19th century, many lawyers did not attend law school. Rules of admission to the bar provided that if a candidate for admission had a college degree, he must regularly study law in the office of a practicing attorney of the Superior Court for three years after receiving such degree. A candidate without a college degree must study law for five years. Napoleon, therefore, would have studied law for a total of five years before presenting himself for the bar exam.

According to the records of the Belknap County Bar Association, Napoleon J. Dyer was admitted to the practice of law in Concord, New Hampshire. The exact date of his admission appears to be March 22, 1889. The Belknap Bar Association has kept a register since 1865, which all newly admitted lawyers sign. Coincidentally, Napoleon J. Dyer was the 18th person to sign the Register of Belknap County lawyers, while his great-grandson, Rodney N. Dyer, was the 71st person to sign. The tradition of having new lawyers sign the register continues to this day. The records are interesting in their own right and include an entry of April 17, 1865, stating that a committee was appointed to "make arrangements relative to a proper observance of the death of President Lincoln, and to draft resolutions."

Napoleon commenced his legal practice by associating with George B. Cox in the law firm known as Cox and Dyer. Cox was a Democrat but, unlike Napoleon, had graduated from Boston University Law School in 1888, with a degree of Bachelor of Law. Cox was also actively involved in the Citizens' Temperance Union, and this may be where Napoleon developed his antipathy toward liquor. He was a teetotaler, and throughout his lifetime actively opposed the use of alcohol.

Napoleon Dyer started practicing law in the wood frame courthouse which had been constructed on Court Street in 1819. He could not have tried many cases in this original structure because in 1893, the Belknap County Convention voted a sum not to exceed $30,000 for the purpose of erecting a new courthouse on the same site. It was dedicated on March 27, 1894, and continues to be used to this day.

Heard in Belknap County Superior Court, in a case involving a horse:

Lawyer [Dyer] to witness: How old was that horse?

Witness: She was seven years old when I bought her three years ago, and that's a good age to sell a horse, so I kept her at seven."

In 1889, the County Trial Court in Belknap County was called the "Supreme Judicial Court." The court was convened twice a year: on the first Tuesday of September and on the first Tuesday of March, at 10:00 in the morning. The sheriff would ring the courthouse bell, summoning jurors, lawyers and litigants to the court. The grand jury would convene, and the lawyers would gather to listen to the call of the docket (a list of cases to be heard at that term of Court). The Belknap County Bar totalled 17 members, including Napoleon J. Dyer as the most recent lawyer admitted to practice. All of the lawyers were, of course, male, and not one French surname was evident. In fact, all of the petit jurors and grand jurors were male, as jurors were selected from voting lists, and only men had the right to vote.

At a meeting of the Belknap County Bar Association on February 17, 1890, in which Napoleon Dyer participated, the following resolution was adopted:

Whereas, the giving of ' street opinions' and gratuitous advice is justly regarded by the Bar generally as tending to lower the dignity of the profession and encourage a species of vagrancy which costs every practicing attorney much valuable time, therefore be it:

Resolved that we, the members of the Belknap County Bar Association, do hereby pledge ourselves to bestow no legal advice without compensation, except in cases where the person seeking such advice is unable by reason of poverty to pay for the same.

President Lincoln was quoted as saying, "a lawyer's time is his stock in trade."

I have in my possession copies of the Belknap County court dockets for 1889 and 1890. Each docket is a printed and bound book with gold lettering on its face, carrying the name of the law firm of Cox & Dyer. The family's oral history is that Napoleon had a penchant for putting notes in the margins of all newspapers and books which he read. This habit is illustrated by the great number of notes he has penciled in the margins of the two printed dockets.

During his career, Napoleon developed a reputation as an able lawyer and a skillful advocate. Apparently, because he learned to read, write and speak English as a second language, he developed a noteworthy eloquence and without an accent. One newspaper article, in commenting upon his fluency, stated that no less an authority than Atty. Harry Lake, prominent member of the bar and ballot law commissioner at Concord, speaks of Atty. Dyer's extensive vocabulary and command of the English language as "truly amazing."

This ability was important in the practice of law, particularly for a litigator. In those days, the favorite defendant was the Boston & Maine Railroad, whose steam engines were constantly running into cows or setting fields and houses afire. Senator Robert Upton, of the Upton law firm in Concord, told me that he recalled trying cases against Napoleon Dyer and found him to be a very skilled lawyer.

Napoleon tried cases in the Superior Court system and argued others in the Supreme Court. One of his most famous cases involved a young woman who threw her baby off the Messer Street Bridge. She told authorities that "God told me to do it." Napoleon developed a legal theory based on irresistible impulse, and the woman was acquitted. This theory was a precursor of later defenses involving findings of innocence because of mental impairment.

Napoleon continued to practice law in the 1920s and, as late as February 1931, was still arguing cases in the New Hampshire Supreme Court. However, his health started to fail, and he took James Doherty into his office; Doherty read the law in Napoleon's office for a period of five years and was one of the last persons to pass the bar without having a law degree. In addition, Napoleon took into his office a young man by the name of Bernard Snierson, and the three practiced law together for a short period of time.

On March 22, 1939, the Belknap County Bar Association celebrated Napoleon's 50th anniversary as a lawyer. At that time, Napoleon was president of the Association, as well as being considered its "dean." According to the newspaper report of the event, *"The banquet was tendered by Justice Oscar L. Young of the Superior Court, a truly graceful gesture of respect and admiration for Atty. Dyer, whose success in acquiring an education and whose fame as a master of pure English require no re-telling. One of the speakers at this gala was Mayor Edward J. Gallagher, who recalled first seeing Atty. Dyer in 1906. The Mayor said he was told by an eminent member of the Bar to note particularly Atty. Dyer's polished diction. Among those attending were Frank Tilton, F.E. Normandin, Attorney General Thomas Cheney, Theo S. Jewett, County Solicitor Harold Wescott, City Solicitor Fred Tilton, Arthur Nighswander, William S. Lord, F.A. Normandin, William W. Keller, Robert V. Johnson, James W. Doherty and Bernard Snierson."*

Napoleon Dyer's career involved more than the practice of law. He was always an enthusiastic Democrat and a zealous worker for his party. He became interested in politics early in his career and was a committed Democrat throughout his entire life.

In 1893, the Town of Laconia was solidly Democrat, and the Republicans of the day chafed over this tradition. Col. Stephen Jewett and other prominent Republicans sponsored a bill in the state legislature which would convert Laconia from a town to a city. It also involved the establishment of wards throughout the city. Since the Irish, French and other ethnic voters who were predominantly Democrats were located within certain defined areas, it was easy to gerrymander the city and end up with a Republican majority. This is exactly what happened, and at the constituent meeting of the City Council in March of 1894, the name of Napoleon Dyer was put forth by the Democrats as Laconia's first City Solicitor, while Col. Stephen Jewett was put forth by the Republicans. Col. Jewett won handily as did all the other Republican nominees, and Laconia remained solidly Republican for a number of years.

In 1898, Napoleon was the Democratic candidate for County Attorney. He lost. Napoleon continued to stay active in Democratic politics, and by 1904, he was the party's nominee for Congress from the First District. According to a contemporary newspaper article, he had always been a staunch Democrat and worked hard in the interest of his party. He had been a supervisor of the checklist and chairman of the City's Democratic Committee for 10 years. His campaign literature in 1904 urged working men to remember Napoleon J. Dyer when they voted. He stated that he " . . . began as a mill boy. As a Knight of Labor and as lawyer my services and advice in your cause have been freely given without price." He styled himself as a self-made man: clean, honest and incorruptible. He worked tirelessly for bi-weekly payments, helped in the struggle to shorten hours of labor, and in the legislature headed the fight against convict-labor. He lost to Cyrus A. Sulloway of Manchester.

Napoleon Dyer's efforts on behalf of the Democratic party were not in vain. President Wilson named Napoleon as Laconia's Postmaster, and he served in that capacity from February 22, 1914, to January 14, 1923. In those days, the office of Postmaster was "the juiciest plum which grows on the political plum tree." Postmaster Dyer's term lasted longer than any other politically appointed Laconia Postmaster. He also presided over the construction of the existing post office at the corner of Beacon Street East and Church Street. Postmaster N.J. Dyer had the *"honor and pleasure of throwing out the first shovelful of dirt"* which marked the breaking of ground for the erection of the new post office on Church and Beacon Streets, April 12, 1917, according to the *Laconia Democrat*. Completion was delayed because of World War I shortages of building materials.

Another family legend is that while Napoleon was mechanically-gifted, he was a notoriously poor automobile driver. This may account for an article in the Citizen dealing with an accident that Napoleon had on Labor Day, 1916. According to the article, *"Postmaster Napoleon J. Dyer and Assistant Postmaster Nat Mitchell figured in an auto accident, Labor Day, 1916, while taking a short joy ride in the Postmaster's car. They were rambling along on Union Avenue when they met a motorcycle chap who was speeding right in the middle of the road and [were] evidently expected to take to the sidewalk. Postmaster Dyer managed to avoid running over the motorbike by steering his gasoline chariot into a telephone pole, but he knocked the other vehicle out from under its rider and wrecked his own machine. The Postmaster and his assistant were thrown out with much violence but were fortunate enough to escape serious injury. Mr. Mitchell sustained a cut on the back of his head and a bloody nose; Mr. Dyer at first thought he had lost one foot but later discovered that it was merely one shoe, which was yanked off his foot by the force of the collision with the telephone pole."*

After his term as postmaster, Napoleon resumed the practice of law and opened an office in the Tilton Block owned by fellow attorney, and later Probate Judge, Frank P. Tilton. Bob Tilton, retired clerk of the Superior Court, recalled that his father once sent him to Napoleon Dyer's office to obtain furniture polish. Napoleon was also an inventor, and he had come up with a formula for furniture polish which Judge Tilton swore was the best in the world. He told his son that Napoleon could have made a fortune with this polish if only he could convince him to market it.

In 1930, Napoleon once again rallied to the call of his party and became the Democratic candidate for Congress from the First District. He lost to Fletcher Hale of Laconia.

Napoleon J. Dyer was a man of average height for his day, approximately 5' 8" or 5' 9". He was not a handsome man, but he was very neat and meticulous. He loved children and cultivated a large garden for many years. He was reputedly a slow speaker, but his words were right to the point. He was a dignified man and was generally called "Mr. Dyer" or "Lawyer Dyer." He was one of those rare individuals who managed to remain vigorous throughout the day with a minimum of sleep, three to four hours a night. According to his grandson, Ronald Dyer, he seldom retired before 3:00 a.m. and was up at 6:00 a.m., refreshed with few hours of sleep. When Ronald was a child, one of his adventures was to stop by Napoleon's law office with his father, George B. Dyer, and rummage through his desk drawers in search of hard candy. Ronald was sure that Napoleon enjoyed watching the search in progress as much as the children enjoyed the candy. Napoleon devoted numerous hours to helping Ronald overcome a pronunciation problem with the letter "r." His methodology was to have Ronald repeat the words "railroad track" until he was satisfied that his appreciation of the sound of the "r" was complete.

Napoleon had interests other than law and politics. According to family members who knew him, he was also very interested in medicine, science and literature. He reportedly corresponded with Albert Einstein and George Bernard Shaw. In fact, one of his children, George Bernard Dyer, was reputedly named after the eminent playwright. Another family member recalls that he would often do physical and chemical experiments. On one occasion, he used cork stoppers to explain the concept of atoms striking one another and multiplying into atomic fission. One should remember that this discussion occurred in the 1930s, long before the advent of the atomic bomb.

Napoleon was also active in civic affairs as witnessed by an article in the *Laconia Democrat* dated March 4, 1892, as follows:

On Friday evening, Folsom Opera House was transformed and made gay by the long anticipated concert and ball of Court Laconia, No. 540, Ancient Order of Foresters of America. If ever any organization had reason to feel proud of their first social, the Foresters have, and well they may, for it drew one of the largest parties that ever gathered within the hall. The ballroom was resplendent with colored bunting and flags. Chief Forester N. J. Dyer and wife led the grand march of nearly one hundred and forty couples, and as the couples marched in and out around the ball to martial music, it made a pretty scene.

The crowded ballroom made the "circle" that was to end the grand march an impossibility.

> *Dancing began soon after 9 o'clock and for three hours it continued, the participants seeming to have only one object in view: to get all the joy possible from the music. The only time the music stopped was when Chief Dyer called Officer Michael J. Whelan to the platform, and on behalf of the Court, presented him with an elegant gold badge emblematic of the order.*

Napoleon Dyer was also somewhat of an eccentric. For example, he continued to cut the hair of his children and grandchildren throughout his lifetime. He was also not bashful about making pronouncements on any subject, as witnessed by an article in the *Citizen*, which stated that:

> *Yesterday's sun spot and storm developments bear out predictions of Atty. Napoleon Dyer, senior member of the Belknap County Bar . . . Atty. Dyer has for the past few years told of the coming storm and has bombarded metropolitan newspapers with letters regarding it. He attributes unusual weather of the past few years to the coming activity of the spots.*

In August 1939, Napoleon spoke on another issue, by publishing in the *Citizen* a letter decrying *"the corruption of youth and the horrible jumble of degrading 'stuff' heard night after night over WLNH, Laconia, NH, which has fired and inflamed the mind of our children with deleterious, debasing and brutalizing tendency for moral rectitude of our youth. We hear on our streets, from the lips of our children anywhere from 5 to 8 or 10 years of age such yells as 'Hi-Yo Silver, the Lone Ranger'. Soon the Green Hornet's droning, then a huddle of brutalized characters doing their stuff."* One can only imagine what Napoleon would think of today's Internet culture.

An interesting insight into his character would be his dispute with the Catholic Church. Napoleon would faithfully transport his wife, Mary Jane, to St. Joseph's Church, but would not enter. Instead he would sit outside in his auto and wait for her. It appears that he had gotten into a philosophical dispute with the parish priest over a portion of the Lord's Prayer, "and lead us not into temptation." According to Napoleon, "My Maker will not lead me into temptation."

He boycotted the church, insisting that the prayer be changed to read "and help to keep us from temptation." This is one battle that Napoleon did not win in spite of his ability to quote the scriptures accurately and at length.

Another losing campaign dealt with leaving ketchup bottles on tables in public diners. Napoleon initiated a campaign to force the diners to remove the ketchup bottles, claiming that they were unsanitary. Once again, his eccentricity met defeat.

Napoleon Dyer appears to have been a man who was whimsical and sometimes eccentric, but at his core he was imbued with a spirit of justice and fought for it all of his life. In the words of Judge Oscar L. Young, "professional reputation and even literary and political fame are ephemeral, but those who knew him will always remember Mr. Dyer as a person of high ideals and strong convictions, a true and worthy example of a self-educated and self-made man."

Napoleon J. Dyer lived in interesting times and proved worthy of his times. In the words of one of his grandchildren, "he was a man of conscience and a man supremely committed to lifelong learning, but also a man of wit and good humor."

The life of Napoleon Dyer was, in many respects, a metaphor for the Franco-American experience in New Hampshire in the late 19th and early 20th centuries. Napoleon came from an impoverished background, but he had a desire to learn and to improve himself. His journey from mill boy to successful professional was difficult but the journey was shared by thousands of others.

Napoleon Dyer was the precursor of other successful professionals, such as members of the Lafrance and Normandin families. People with French surnames, such as Morin, Breton, St. Pierre, Bisson, Gilbert and Levasseuer became owners of successful businesses. People with names such as Huot and D'Amours could actually be elected to Congress, while countless others became selectmen, aldermen, mayors and state legislators.

Franco-Americans have now successfully assimilated into all facets of business, commerce and society. The assimilation has had a price in the loss of the French language, culture and traditions, but this is the price that all cultures must pay in order to become part of the American experience.

Napoleon's spelling book—stamped March 27, 1917

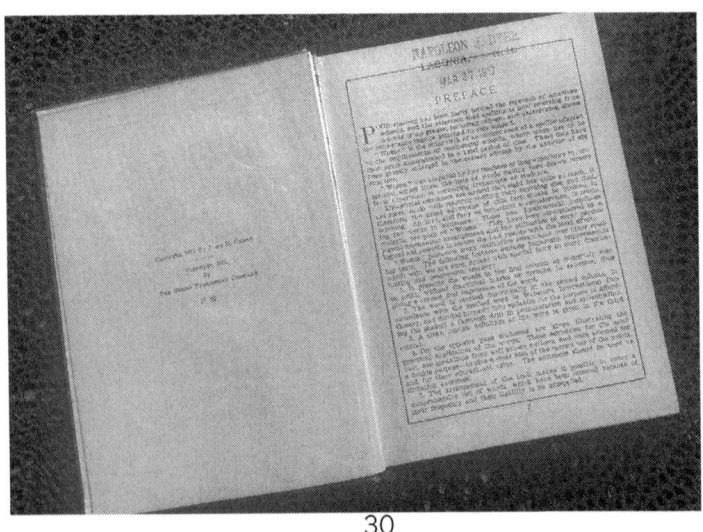

Belknap County Bar.

Ellery A. Hibbard	Laconia	July, 1849
Samuel W. Rollins	Meredith	Aug., 1849
Samuel C. Clark	Lake Village	1854
Charles C. Rogers	Tilton	1858
Woodbury L. Melcher	Laconia	Sept., 1861
Erastus P. Jewell	Laconia	Mar., 1865
Thomas Cogswell	Gilmanton I. W.	Sept., 1866
Charles F. Stone	Laconia	Mar., 1872
Edwin P. Thompson	Belmont	Mar., 1876
Charles B. Hibbard	Laconia	Aug., 1879
John W. Ashman	Laconia	Mar., 1880
Stephen S. Jewett	Laconia	Mar., 1880
Clarence H. Pearson	Laconia	1882
William B. Fellows	Tilton	Aug., 1883
Edwin H. Shannon	Gilmanton I. W.	Mar.,
Walter S. Peaslee	Laconia	Aug., 1885
George B. Cox	Laconia	
Napoleon J. Dyer	Laconia	Mar., 1889
William A. Plummer	Laconia	Aug., 1889
Frank M. Beckford	Laconia	Aug., 1889

Belknap County Bar list

Napoleon always fought for what he believed in.

Bar Association, 1894

Front Row (left to right)
Napoleon J. Dyer, Walter S. Peaslee, George B. Cox, William A. Plummer and Charles B. Hibbard

Middle Row:
Stephen S. Jewett (standing), WB Fellows, Edwin P. Thompson, President of Belknap County Bar Association Ellery A. Hibbard, and Woodbury L. Melcher, Sr.

Top Row:
Thomas Cogswell and Frank M. Beckford (standing), the next three seated are most likely visiting judges or justices attending the dedication of the new Belknap County Court House, then standing to right are Judge Charles F. Stone (holding derby) and Erastus P. Jewell

Belknap County Dockets, 1889

OBER 12, 1965

Dinner Given Napoleon Dyer, Lawyer 50 Years

March 22, 1939

Fifty years a member of the New Hampshire bar. That's the record of Atty. Napoleon J. Dyer, former postmaster.

Judge Trapp said it was rare indeed to establish a record of 50 years service in anything.

Except for the fact that gold had been taken out of circulation beyond the requirements for filling teeth and making wedding rings, the next best thing Judge Trapp said the members of the bar had decided to present him a pot of silver.

A money bag containing $58 all but two of which were silver cartwheels was emptied in a pile before Atty. Dyer who completely overcome sat with tears streaming unashamedly down his cheeks.

His fame as a master of pure English requires no re-telling.

50th anniversary article—March 22, 1939

Postmaster Napoleon Dyer (front row, third from the left) with staff at start of construction of the Laconia Post Office.

New Laconia Post Office—constructed 1917-1919

Laconia Postmaster Napoleon Dyer with Assistant Postmaster Charles F. Shastany (Circa 1920)

Postmaster Dyer with his soon to be wrecked automobile at the Laconia Post Office.

Page 4 Evening Citizen, Laconia, N.H. Saturday, December 24, 1988

Our Yesterdays

By GILBERT S. CENTER

100 YEARS AGO (1888)
from The Laconia Democrat
At a recent session of the Belknap County Teachers Institute held in Meredith Village, Professor Patterson's report revealed that out of $111,392 invested in school property, Laconia had $47,000 "including one house unfit for use." Salaries for female teachers in Laconia averaged $39.50 per month, while the average for the county was $25.97. While total expenditures for the county were $44,103.54, Laconia spent $21,373.15. The average cost per pupil was $9.48.

75 YEARS AGO (1913)
from The Laconia Democrat
Napoleon J. Dyer was named to succeed Julian F. Trask as postmaster. The Troy, N.Y., native came to Laconia in 1876. After being employed for a time as a dyer in the mills, he engaged in business for himself as a barber. Determined to get an education, he attended St. Joseph's parish parochial school during his spare hours, studied under private tutors and took a Chautauqua course until he started reading law in the office of Col. S.S. Jewett and later with Jewett & Stone, being admitted to the bar in 1889. Devoting himself to politics, he became a member of the Democratic city and state committees. "The Laconia postmastership carries a salary of $2600 a year and is the juiciest 'plum' which grows on the political plum-tree. That Mr. Dyer will make an efficient postmaster, nobody we think will undertake to dispute...."

"A notable addition" to Union Cemetery was the granite and marble mausoleum erected by Mrs. Charles A. Busiel. The structure was understood to have cost $12,000. The body of the late governor had been placed there and the remains of his daughter, Frances Busiel Smith, and her son, Charles Busiel Smith, had been brought from Philadelphia.

50 YEARS AGO (1938)
from The Evening Citizen
"One of the most interesting

New Postmaster
Napoleon J. Dyer succeeded Julian F. Trask as Laconia postmaster, 75 years ago this week. Rising from humble beginnings, Dyer achieved prominence as a lawyer and Democratic party official.

little dramas of the Salvation Army Christmas Kettles is that of the Mysterious Mr., Mrs. or Miss who like Santa Claus moves so quickly and quietly that he leaves the gift and is always away before noticed. "On Saturday a mysterious person placed three ten dollar bills in the Salvation Army Kettle and was gone...."

Postmaster Michael J. Carroll announced that although there would be no mail deliveries on Christmas Day and Monday, parcel post packages would be distributed so that no gifts would be late if the post office could help it.

High scorer in the Christmas Eve game between the Battery C sharpshooters and the New Order of Allegiance Club of Manchester on the local armory court was Jimmy Noucas. The lively NOA forward was a counterman at the Crystal Cafe during the previous summer season.

At the weekly Leavitt Park Social Club dance on Christmas Eve, Mrs. Dorothy Kelly Weiler of the Bouve Boston School of Physical Education taught those attending the Lambeth Walk. Ellen Holt, home from Middlebury College, played the piano.

25 YEARS AGO (1963)
from The Evening Citizen
Laconia High School's Good Citizen was Susan Schwass. She would be sponsored by Mary Butler Chapter, Daughters of the American Revolution, in the annual competition for a New Hampshire Good Citizen.

The Rev. Robert G. Hinckley accepted a call to the South Baptist Church. He would commence his new duties Jan. 30.

The so-called modern math "which isn't really so modern," was being taught in the first three grades in the Laconia elementary schools and was to be studied in the fourth grade the next year. It was also being taught in the senior high school.

Scott Colbath, a French teacher at Laconia High School, was named coordinator of the newly-installed language laboratory in Room 106. French and Spanish classes would begin using the facility in January.

10 YEARS AGO (1978)
from The Evening Citizen
A Christmas Day storm dropped 11½ inches of snow on the Lakes Region. Accompanied by strong winds, the storm kept highway and utility crews busy. Power outages occurred in Belmont, Moultonboro, Ossipee and Sandwich.

Browning Laboratories, a citizen's band radio manufacturer that opened its doors 20 years earlier, was to close them at the end of the year. Gardiner G. Greene Jr., president of the company, explained that the whole CB industry was in trouble. The firm had 20 employees. They voted to give $533.93 profits from vending machines in the plant to the Santa Fund.

At a dinner honoring LHS cross-country and golf teams, Russ Lagueux was named runner of the year and Neil Colstad and Pat Hebert the most improved runners. The Bud Levasseur Memorial Fund provided jackets for the golf team.

Robert B. MacHaffie, 48, died. A landscape architect with the U.S. Forest Service, he had been with the White Mountain National Forest for 17 years, was Forest Service representative on the Mount Washington Summit Building Committee and a member of the planning commission of the state Forest History Museum.

The very best for the

Our Yesterdays article—Laconia Citizen

Dionne Family Crest

N. H., WEDNESDAY, OCTOBER 27, 1943

ERY BAND
~~ARADE TOMORROW~~

will roll into town tomorrow
gdon, Portsmouth, for the
Army" to be given at the

e state armory at 2:30 pro-
to Main street.

Coast Artillery crack band,
There will be at least ten
anager Ralph Morris of the

n at three in front of the
the things pictured on the
n the performance will be
rmy Emergency Relief fund.

Senior Member of
County Bar Dies

(Continued from Page 1)
and followed it with, "I will be one
day."

His fine power of reasoning and his
nice choice of words was evident
and he was given encouragement by
the leaders of the bar who saw that
he was serious.

Being unable to read and write
was a handicap that would have
stopped many a man but he started
to learn. His next job was as a
weaver in one of the mills and he
told of a woman there who wrote
the words in chalk on the cloth. He
used to copy them.

After work as soon as he had mas-
tered reading and writing Mr. Dyer
began reading law in the office of
the late Col. Stephen S. Jewett and
he was afterwards associated with
the office of Jewell and Stone.

Mr. Dyer was appointed postmaster Feb. 22, 1914, and served until
Jan. 15, 1923.

He returned to his office in the
Tilton building when his term as
postmaster was over.

Atty James W. Doherty studied
law with Mr. Dyer and the two became associated together when the
younger man passed the bar examin-
ations. Later Atty. Bernard Snierson, now an officer in the army, en-
tered the firm and Mr. Dyer became
consultant for some years.

The two younger members of the
bar then opened their own offices.

A few years ago the County Bar
association which Mr. Dyer had
served as president honored him at
a dinner in honor of a half century
at the bar.

Mr. Dyer leaves his widow, Mrs.
Mary J. Dyer who is now of Belmont,
Mass., two sons, John A. and George
R. of Laconia; a daughter, Mrs. Marie
Wilson of Belmont, Mass.; 19 grand-
children, 14 great grandchildren; a
half brother Frank L. Lavigne of
Brockton, Mass. and nephews and
nieces.

NAPOLEON J. DYER
SENIOR MEMBER OF
COUNTY BAR, DIES

Atty. Napoleon J. Dyer senior
member of the Belknap county bar.

NAPOLEON J. DYER

died this morning at a hospital in
Concord after a long period of failing
health.

The body was removed to the Wil-
kinson Funeral home. Mass of Re-
quiem will be offered Saturday morning at eight at St. Joseph's church.
Burial will be in St. Lambert cemetery.

Napoleon J. Dyer was born May
24, 1858, in Troy, N. Y., the son of
Joseph and Katherine Brodeur. He
had lived in Laconia for more than
70 years.

He was at first a barber and used
to like to discuss cases with the
lawyers of his younger days.

"If I was a lawyer," he would say
(continued on page 2)

GUNSTOCK HILL FARMS
CHANGE HANDS

John F. Weeks, local dairyman, and
his wife have purchased from Albert
W. Von Lilienthal, of Beacon, N. Y.,
administrator of the estate of Frances
Von Lilienthal, the large Von Lilienthal farm at the crest of Gunstock
Hill in Gilford.

The view is one of the most beauti-
ful in the whole county overlooking
Lake Winnipesaukee and the smaller
lakes and the mountains beyond. The
buildings and a number of tracts of
land are included.

Malcolm Harrington of Province
street has leased for a period of five
years from Mrs. May Whitcomb and
Walter McLennan of Weston, Mass.,
the Whitcomb Farms at the foot of
the hill bordering on the Lake Shore
road. He has had a crew of men
picking apples there.

Napoleon Dyer: Obituary

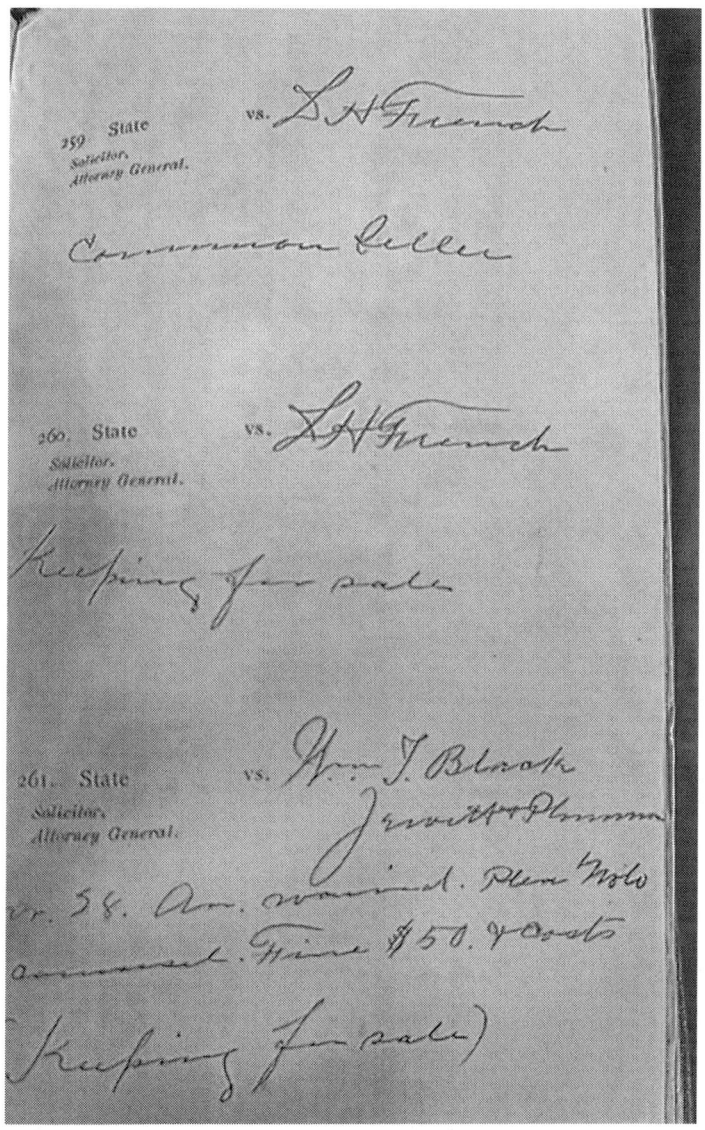

Napoleon Dyer's notes in his Belknap Court Docket for the March Term, 1890.

Gravesite—St Lambert Cemetery, Laconia, NH

About the Author

Rod Dyer was born in Laconia, NH, in 1936. He lost his dad in 1944, who was a member of the 25th Marines and was killed in action in the South Pacific. As a war orphan, Rod was entitled to attend the University of New Hampshire (UNH) tuition free, including free room and board.

He went on to Boston University (BU) Law using scholarships and his father's GI Bill. He passed the bar in 1961 and joined the firm of James Doherty (the same person who had prepared for the bar in Napoleon Dyer's law office). Joining the Wescott & Millham firm in Laconia in 1964, he remained with the firm until his retirement in December 2021.

Rod has served as Laconia's city attorney, school board chair, and two terms as mayor. He has received awards from a number of community organizations, and New Hampshire Bar Foundation. He is Chairman Emertius of the Bank of New Hampshire.

He and his wife, Gail, live at the Taylor Community in Laconia. They have two adult children, grandchildren and great-grandchildren.

About the Belknap Mill

The Belknap Mill is the oldest, largely unaltered, brick textile mill in the United States. Built in 1823, it is one of America's oldest surviving textile mills and was a leader in what would become the standard for American manufacturing. The subsequent success of the textile hosiery industry in Laconia and surrounding towns drew inventors and machine manufacturers to Laconia. In 1861, during the Civil War, the Belknap Mill was one of the first mills to convert from weaving to knitting, and through both World Wars the Mill provided socks to our soldiers around the world. Socks continued to be made at the Belknap Mill until 1969. The building was scheduled to be demolished by the City of Laconia as part of a plan to revitalize downtown, when a group of citizens acting under the banner of 'Save the Mill Society,' purchased the building. Because of the national significance of the Mill, the group worked with historic preservationists across the country to save and maintain the building as a cultural community center.

The Belknap Mill has served as an art and history center and meeting place since being saved in the early 1970's. In a nationally covered scenario, the private nonprofit, cultural organization was the first in the country to be awarded Federal funds as well as recognition from the National Trust for Historic Preservation for preserving an industrial structure.

Today the Belknap Mill offers a permanent exhibit on industrial history, changing exhibits on art and history, and education programs for adults and children along with workshops, lectures, festivals, and other events, year-round. The Society's programs, preservation projects, community service and management have won national and state awards. The Belknap Mill is known as the Official Meetinghouse of New Hampshire, designated by a former governor for its architectural, geographical, and historical significance.

The Belknap Mill Society operates as a 501(c)(3) nonprofit organization, whose mission is to preserve the Belknap Mill as a unique historic gathering place and to celebrate the Lakes Region's cultural heritage.

Made in the USA
Middletown, DE
08 October 2022

12217340R00029